Cornelia Clapp

Manual of gymnastics

Prepared for the use of the students of Mt. Holyoke Seminary

Cornelia Clapp

Manual of gymnastics
Prepared for the use of the students of Mt. Holyoke Seminary

ISBN/EAN: 9783337281274

Printed in Europe, USA, Canada, Australia, Japan

Cover: Foto ©Paul-Georg Meister /pixelio.de

More available books at **www.hansebooks.com**

MANUAL OF GYMNASTICS

Prepared for the Use of the Students of

MT. HOLYOKE SEMINARY

By Cornelia M. Clapp

Instructor in Gymnastics

1883

THE DIO LEWIS SYSTEM.

GENERAL PRINCIPLES.

POSITION. — Heels together ; toes out, so that the feet may form a right angle ; head erect ; shoulders and hips drawn back ; hands naturally at sides, unless otherwise specified.

TIME. — The system of numbering in the exercises is this : each strain consists of eight accented and eight unaccented beats, or what in marching would be eight steps with the left foot and eight steps with the right, and time is kept by counting the numerals from one to eight for the heavy beats, and for the light beats the syllable "and." The pupil always resumes, on the unaccented beat, the position with which he began the last preceding accented beat.

FREE GYMNASTICS.

These exercises are performed without apparatus. They are arranged in three series of equal length, and a chorus, so that, when a class shall have become sufficiently proficient, each of the three series may be performed at the same time, by different portions of the class, and the chorus by the class all together. Hands firmly closed and well back upon the chest. All thrusts are from the chest unless otherwise specified.

FIRST SERIES.

HAND MOVEMENTS.

1. Thrust right hand down from chest twice ; left twice ; simultaneous twice.

2. Repeat No. 1, thrusting out at side.

3. Repeat No. 1, thrusting up.

4. Repeat No. 1, thrusting in front.

5. Right hand down once ; left once ; drum beat (right a little in advance of left) once ; simultaneous once ; same out at sides.

6. Repeat No. 5, thrusting up and in front.

7. Right hand down once ; left once ; clap hands ; same out at sides.

8. Repeat No. 7, thrusting up and in front.

FOOT MOVEMENTS.

9. Hands on hips ; divide a circle about the body, with a radius of from two to three feet, into eight equal parts, by stepping forward, diagonal forward, at side, diagonal back, etc., with right foot, keeping left knee straight and the feet at right angles, except last two steps, bending right knee each step.

10. Repeat No. 9 with left foot.

11. Same movement, alternating right and left.

12. Charge diagonal forward with right foot, advancing with three steps, bending right knee, left straight ; same on the left side ; same diagonal back on right side ; same left.

13. Repeat No. 12. Foot movements always performed quite slowly, with very slow time. "*Music in the Air*" is best.

BODY MOVEMENTS.

14. Hands on hips; twist upper body half round to right, then to left, alternately, stopping in front on unaccented beats.

15. Bend upper body to right and left.

16. Bend forward and back.

17. Bend body to right, back, left, front; then reverse, bending to left, back, right, front; repeat, becoming erect only on last beat.

HEAD MOVEMENTS.

18. Same as 14, except that the head alone is moved.

19. Same as 15, except that the head alone is moved.

20. Same as 16, except that the head alone is moved.

21. Same as 17, except that the head alone is moved.

MISCELLANEOUS MOVEMENTS.

22. Arms extended in front, thumbs up, raise hands about a foot, and bring forcibly to shoulders.

23. Arms horizontal in front; raise right hand to perpendicular over head twice; left twice; alternate twice, and simultaneous twice.

24. Thrust hands down, out at sides, up, in front, twisting the arms at each thrust; repeat.

25. Repeat No. 24.

26. Thrust hands to floor, not bending knees; then over head, rising on toes, opening hands at each thrust.

27. Hands at sides open; swing them over head, clapping them, at same time stepping right foot to left, and left foot to right, alternately.

28. Stamp left foot, then right; then charge diagonal forward with right; bend and straighten right knee; at same time throwing arms back from horizontal in front.

29. Repeat No. 28 on left side.

SECOND SERIES.

HAND MOVEMENTS.

1. Thrust right hand down and up alternately.
2. Repeat No. 1 with left hand.
3. Alternate, right going down as left goes up, and *vice versa.*
4. Simultaneous, both down, then both up, etc.
5. Thrust right hand to right and left, alternately, twisting body when thrusting to left.
6. Thrust left hand to left, and right, twisting to right.
7. Thrust both hands alternately to right and left, twisting body.
8. Thrust both hands to right four times, to left four times.

FOOT MOVEMENTS.

9. Hands on hips; kick diagonal forward with right foot, three times, stamping floor on fourth beat; same with left.
10. Kick diagonal back three times with right foot, same with left.
11. Repeat No. 9.
12. Repeat No. 10.

ARM MOVEMENTS.

13. Hands down at sides; raise stiff right arm forward over head four times; left four times.
14. Alternate four times; simultaneous four times.
15. Raise stiff right arm sidewise over head four times; left four times.

16. Alternate four times ; simultaneous four times.

17. Arms extended in front; swing them back horizontally.

SHOULDER MOVEMENTS.

18. Hands at sides ; raise right shoulder four times; left four times.

19. Alternate four times ; simultaneous four times.

MISCELLANEOUS MOVEMENTS.

20. Hands down at sides ; open hands and spread fingers four times ; out at sides four times.

21. Hands up ; open four times ; in front four times.

22. Mowing movement from right to left, and left to right.

23. Hands on hips ; throw elbows back.

24. Bend body down diagonal to right, and thrust right and left hands down alternately as near the floor as possible, four beats ; same bending diagonally to left side.

25. Repeat No. 24.

26. Swing arms around in front, clasping shoulders, right hand above, then left above, alternately.

27. Hands on hips ; stamp left foot, then right foot ; charge diagonal forward with right, sway the body, bending right and left knees alternately.

28. Repeat No. 27, diagonal forward on the left side.

29. Repeat diagonal back on the right side.

30. Repeat diagonal back on the left.

THIRD SERIES.

ATTITUDES AND PERCUSSION.

1. Hands on hips ; stamp left foot, then right ; charge diagonal forward with right foot ; inflate the lungs.

2. Remaining in the attitude, percuss the upper part of the chest.

3. Repeat No. 1, diagonal forward left.

4. Repeat No. 2.

5. Repeat No. 1, diagonal back right side.

6. Percuss the lower part of the chest.

7. Repeat No. 1, diagonal back, left side.

8. Repeat No. 7.

HAND MOVEMENTS.

9. Hands clasped behind the back ; raise and thrust down.

10. Hands down at sides, thumbs out ; twist hands half round, four beats ; hands out at sides, thumbs back, twist hands half round.

11. Hands above the head, thumbs in, twist hands half round ; hands in front, thumbs out, twist hands half round.

12. Palms together in front, slide right and left hand forward alternately, elbows straight.

SHOULDER MOVEMENTS.

13. Hands down at sides ; describe forward circle with right shoulder four times ; left four times.

14. Alternate four times ; simultaneous four times.

15. Repeat No. 13, making backward circle.
16. Repeat No. 14, making backward circle.

ARM MOVEMENTS.

17. Fists in arm-pits ; thrust right hand down four times ; left four times.
18. Alternate four times ; simultaneous four times.
19 Fists upon the shoulders; thrust right hand up four times ; left four times.
20. Alternate four times ; simultaneous four times.
21. Right hand down from arm-pit, and left up from shoulder four times ; left down from arm-pit, and right up from shoulder four times.
22. Alternately right down and left up, and left down and right up, one strain.
23. Simultaneous, both down, then both up, one strain.
24. Hands down at sides ; raise right hand to horizontal in front, four times ; left four times.
25. Alternate four times ; simultaneous four times.
26. Hands over head ; sway body to right and left alternately.

ATTITUDES.

27. Hands on hips, stamp left foot, then right ; charge diagonal forward with right, looking over left shoulder. -
28. Repeat No. 27, diagonal forward left foot.
29. Repeat No. 27, diagonal back right.
30. Repeat No. 27, diagonal back left.

CHORUS.

Music — " *Yankee Doodle* " (*always*).

1. Repeat No. 1, first series.

2. Clap hands.

3. Percuss chest.

4. Hop on right foot, eight times ; left eight times.

5. Repeat No. 2, first series.

6. Clap hands.

7. Percuss chest.

8. Leap right and left foot alternately eight times, both together eight times.

9. Repeat No. 3, first series.

10. Clap hands.

11. Percuss chest.

12. Leap right and left foot alternately in front and back (long step) one strain.

13. Repeat No. 4, first series.

14. Clap hands.

15. Percuss chest.

16. Crossing feet one strain.

WAND EXERCISES.

In these exercises the hands are placed upon the hips, unless occupied in holding the wand. The wand is held at the right shoulder. First signal, pass the wand over in front, grasping it with the left hand, so that the wand becomes horizontal in front of the body. Second signal, raise the wand until the arms become horizontal in front of the body ; place the hands so as to divide the wand into three equal parts. Third signal, bring the hands back to sides.

1. Raise the wand to chin four times ; keeping elbows high, last time carry it above the head ; bring wand from above the head to chin four times.

2. Bring wand from above the head to the floor four times without bending knees or elbows; to back of the neck four times.

3. Bring wand from above the head to chin, and back of the neck, alternately, four times each.

4. Wand above the head; on first heavy beat, carry right hand to right end of wand; second, carry left to left end; then carry wand back of the head to hips six times, keeping elbows straight.

5. Carry wand from above the head to front as near the floor as possible, and back of the head to hips, four times each.

6. Carry wand from above the head to right and left sides alternately, bringing it to a perpendicular position; elbows straight. Do this on half time.

7. First heavy beat, let go of the wand with the left hand, placing end of wand upon the floor between the feet; second, place it diagonally forward on the right side, the length of the arm; charge the right foot to the wand six times; keeping right arm and left leg straight, and wand perpendicular and still.

8. *Vice versa* on left side.

9. Repeat No. 7, with longer charge, and, the charging foot remaining stationary, the knee bends and straightens.

10. *Vice versa* on left side; turning the left hand thumb down on first beat; bring wand into position for No. 11.

11. Arms horizontal in front, wand perpendicular, bring hands to chest eight times, elbows high.

12. Arms and wand same position, bring wand to right shoulder and left, alternately, four times each.

13. Hands upon front of chest; point the wand diagonally forward, right and left alternately, 45 degrees.

14. Pointing wand diagonally forward, right and left, first strain, and diagonally backward second strain, charge diagonally forward right, diagonally forward left, diagonally backward left, diagonally backward right, diagonally forward left,

diagonally forward right, diagonally backward right, diagonally backward left; four strains in all, first two wand points forward, last two wand points back. Move on half time.

15. Wand horizontal over head, right hand front, left back; reverse, twist half time through half a strain.

16. Wand the same, right face; bend over, bringing the wand to a perpendicular on right side, right hand up, four times.

17. Same movement on left side.

18. Same movement, alternately right and left.

19. First heavy beat, place left end of wand upon the floor at the feet; second, place it directly in front, the length of the arm; charge right foot to the wand three times, left three times.

20. Charge right foot backward four times, left four times.

21. Right foot forward and back, same step, four times, left same.

22. Rest first half of strain; last half, charge right foot forward, same time left back, left forward, right back, etc.

23. Face the front, carry the wand from perpendicular in front of right shoulder, left hand up, to perpendicular in front of left shoulder, right hand up, four times; fourth time carry it from front to back of left, then carry it from back of left to back of right four times, fourth time from back of right to front of right.

24. Carry wand around the body from front of right to front of left, back of left, back of right, front of right, repeat, then reverse.

25. Carry the wand from front of right to back of left four times; from front of left to back of right four times.

26. Right face; place left end of wand upon the floor, charge with right foot to the right side, back, to the left side behind the left leg, same in front of left leg; *vice versa* left.

27. Same movement as No. 26, right and left alternately.

28. Face the front, wand in front of chest, right hand down, bring left down, right down, etc., four beats ; same movement, wand behind the center of the back.

29. Wand back of center of head, charge diagonally forward right foot, raising right end of wand 45 degrees, then diagonally forward left, raising left end of wand 45 degrees. This is done the first half of strain during the last half charge, in same manner, only turn the body more sidewise, keeping wand straight over head.

30. Wand down horizontal in front, on first beat thrust perpendicular on right side, next beat same on left, so on through half strain. Last half in same manner, only charge right and left every time the wand is raised horizontally left.

31. First half of strain same as first half of last exercise ; last half throw wand horizontally over the head on every charge.

DUMB BELL EXERCISES.

In the attitudes of these exercises the bells are first brought to the chest, and then, unless otherwise specified, are placed upon the hips.

FIRST SERIES.

FIRST SET.

1. Bells down at sides, and in same horizontal line, palms front, turn out-ends in four times. *Attitude.* — Charge right foot diagonally forward, looking over right shoulder ; head, shoulders, hips and left heel, in diagonal line.

2. Elbows on hips, bells forward and in line, turn out-ends

in four times. *Attitude.*—Charge left foot diagonally forward, look over left shoulder.

3. Bells extended at sides and parallel, palms up, turn four times. *Attitude.*—Charge right foot diagonally back, and look over right shoulder.

4. Bells extended up, palms front, turn four times. *Attitude.*—Charge left foot diagonally back, and look over left shoulder.

SECOND SET.

5. Bells at chest, thrust down, out at sides, up, and in front. *Attitude.*—Twist body to the right, knees straight, bells extended up over head.

6. Repeat No. 5, except twist body to the left.

7. Bells down at sides, bring right hand to arm-pit twice, left twice, alternate twice, and both twice.

8. Bells on shoulders, thrust right up, left up, both twice. *Attitude.*—Stand on toes, bells over head and parallel.

THIRD SET.

9. Bells extended in front, palms up, turn four times. *Attitude.*—Charge right foot diagonally forward, and look at left bell, which is extended.

10. Right bell up, palm in front, left bell out at side, palm up, turn four times. *Attitude.*—Charge left foot diagonally forward, and look at right bell, which is extended.

11. Left bell up. right bell out at side, turn four times. *Attitude.*—Charge right foot diagonally back, both bells over head.

12. Arms obliquely up at sides, palms up, turn four times. *Attitude.*—Charge left foot diagonally back, both bells over head.

FOURTH SET.

13. Bells on chest, thrust right hand down, then up, then left down and up. *Attitude.* —Twist body to the right, thrust right arm obliquely up, left obliquely down, palms up.

14. Thrust right down, left up, left down, right up, then both down, both up. *Attitude.*— Same as attitude No. 13, except twisting to left, etc.

15. Thrust right in front, left front, both front twice. *Attitude.*— Long side charge with right foot, left resting on toe, bells above the head ; arms, head, shoulders, hips, and left heel, in same oblique plane, bells parallel.

16. Bells out in front and vertical, swing both 90 degrees to right and back, left and back, repeat. *Attitude.*— Same as attitude No. 15, except on left side, etc. 17. Wing.

17. Bells in front, bring forcibly to chest four times. *Attitude.*— Arms folded, bells on chest, bend body back.

SECOND SERIES.

Music — "*Grand Russian March.*"

FIRST SET.

18. Stamp left foot, then right, charge at the side with right foot, right arm obliquely up, palm up, left obliquely down, palm down, bend and straighten right knee twice ; *vice versa* on left side.

19. Bells down and parallel at sides, swing right bell up, forward over head twice, left twice, alternate twice, simultaneous twice.

20. Side charge to right, right bell up, left on shoulder, sway the body as in No. 18 ; *vice versa* on left side.

21. Bells down at side, swing right bell up sidewise over head twice, left twice, alternate twice, simultaneous twice.

22. Side charge to right, both bells over head, sway the body twice ; *vice versa* left.

SECOND SET.

23. Hands clasping bells together, describe circle over head from right to left, and from left to right, alternating.

THIRD SET.

24. Stamp left, then right, long diagonal charge to right ; position as in attitude of No. 15, bring bells to shoulder and thrust up ; *vice versa* left.

25. Bells vertical and parallel under chin, throw elbows back horizontally.

FOURTH SET.

26. Stamp left foot, then right, place right diagonally forward a little, swing bells forward, over head, back 90 degrees, then touch floor ; *vice versa* on left side.

27. Stamp left foot, then right, charge directly sidewise right, right bell upon hip, left at side ; swing left up over head.

28. Same, charging sidewise with left foot.

29. Bells extended in front and vertical, swing arms back horizontally.

FIFTH SET.

30. Stamp left foot, then right, charge diagonally forward right, bells over head, bring to shoulder and return ; *vice versa* left.

31. Elbows on hips, arms vertical at sides, twist four beats,

then from chest thrust forward alternately two beats, and simultaneously two beats.

32. Charge diagonally backward with right foot, bells as in No. 30 ; *vice versa* left.

SIXTH SET.

33. Grasp armful horizontally with right arm twice, left twice, alternate twice, simultaneous twice.

34. Twist body to right, then left, swinging bells over head.

35. Thrust bells to floor, then thrust them up, standing on toes.

36. Bells on shoulders, thrust right out at side, palms up twice ; left twice, alternate twice, simultaneous twice.

37. Bells from shoulder to chest, thrust forward, raise over head, return to front, touch floor, back to front, etc.

SEVENTH SET.

38. French Sword. Stamp left, then right, then mark time two beats with right, then charge right two beats, right arm extended, left in curve over head.

39. Same on other side with left, eight beats ; alternate eight beats.

EIGHTH SET.

40. Thrust left bell diagonally backward up 45 degrees, right bell upon hip, advance right foot diagonally forward with four stamps, turning left bell each step ; *vice versa* left.

41. First strain charge diagonally forward right and left alternately, thrusting left and right bells diagonally back ; second strain charge at side right and left alternately, arms in same position as in No. 18, two beats, then arms as in No. 22, two beats.

NINTH SET.

42. Bells on chest, thrust right bell forward, swing right arm back in horizontal plane, half strain ; same left.

43. Alternately eight beats, turn body to right, right arm extended, swing clear round to left ; then, left arm extended, swing round to right, continue eight times.

TENTH SET.

44. Side charge to right, right arm extended, bell vertical, left bell swung vertically over in circle twice, bending right and left knees alternately ; *vice versa* left.

ANVIL CHORUS.

Music — "*Anvil Chorus*" (always).

1. Left bell in front, right back of the neck, swing right bell overhead to front, striking left bell, left swings down and back to position behind the neck, right remaining in front ; repeat the same, swinging over left bell ; same, swinging right bell down by side, striking left from under instead of over ; same left.

2. Repeat No. 1, over one strain, underneath one strain.

3. Diagonal charges in front, without stamping, first with right foot, then left.

4. Repeat No. 1.

5. Repeat No. 3, except charging diagonally backward.

6. Repeat No. 1.

7. Striking bells in front and behind twice, then overhead and behind.

8. Repeat No. 1.

9. Charges. Stamp right foot on first beat, step out diagonally on " and," strike bell overhead on " two," back to position, with bells at sides on " and." Repeat with left foot.

. 10. On " and " after " four " turn directly to the right and repeat No. 9.

11. Repeat No. 9, facing the opposite end of the hall.

12. Repeat No. 9, turning still to right.

13. Repeat No. 9, facing front again.

14. Repeat No. 1.

15. Strike bells in front and behind.

16. Repeat No. 1.

17. Regular anvil to right.

18. Repeat No. 1.

19. Regular anvil to left.

20. Repeat No. 1.

21. Right bell under arm, left on shoulder. Bells down and up from shoulders.

22. Repeat No. 1.

23. Striking bells over head with both lobes.

24. Repeat No. 1.

25. Diagonal charge front with right foot, back with right foot, left foot diagonally back and left foot diagonally front.

26. Repeat No. 1.

RING EXERCISES.

These exercises are performed by couples. Partners stand at commencement about three feet apart, facing each other, the one at right of teacher on the platform holding both rings.

FIRST SERIES.

FIRST SET.

1. On first beat the ring in right hand is presented in a vertical plane, and grasped by right hand of partner; second, right toes are placed together; third, left feet step back, and left hands are placed upon hips, ring is turned into a horizontal plane, turn the ring the other side up and back the remainder of the number.

2. Same movement, except left for right, and *vice versa*.

3. Same as No. 1, except both hands hold rings.

4. Same as No. 3, except left toes are together.

SECOND SET.

5. First, turn back to back; second, place left feet together; third, charge out with right, turn rings through number.

6. First, place right feet together; second, charge out with left, turn rings.

7. First, turn face to face; second, raise arms above the head, bend down and touch rings to floor, not bending knees, twice; arms above the head, bring them down to sides alternately two beats, simultaneous two beats.

THIRD SET.

8. First, turn back to back; second, left face, place hands on shoulders, thrust up, out at sides, down, twice each.

9. Thrust up, out, down, once each through eight beats.

FOURTH SET.

10. First, left face; second, turn face to face; third, place left foot inside of left of partner; fourth, right foot back and

right hand to right shoulder; left to partner's right shoulder, pull back and forth.

11. Same with right feet together, etc.

12. Rest first half of strain; last half, right foot and hand forward same time, left back, left forward, right back, etc.

FIFTH SET.

13. First, back to back, charge diagonal forward right and left alternately.

SIXTH SET.

14. First, face to face; second, right foot inside right of partner's; third, left feet step back. Rings over head, arms stiff, sway alternately through strain.

15. Same with left feet together.

SEVENTH SET.

16. First, back to back, charge up and down the hall alternately, twice each, alternately right feet at same time, left same.

17. First, face to face, charge same as No. 16.

18. First, back to back; second, right face; third, step about two feet apart, raise outside arms and inside arms alternately and simultaneously, change on five.

SECOND SERIES.

FIRST SET.

19. First, left face; second, turn face to face; third, spring apart, placing right feet pointing toward each other, left back

at right angles with right, right hands grasping rings, charge with right feet to right side of partner, stopping suddenly at horizontal plane when coming to position.

20. Same, using right for left, and left for right.

21. Same, holding rings in both hands, and charging right and left alternately, right foot to left side of partner, left to right.

SECOND SET.

22. First, approach ; second, turn back to back ; third, place left feet together ; fourth, step out with right, touch shoulders, arms horizontal.

23. Same, using right for left, and left for right.

THIRD SET.

24. First, face to face ; second, left face, swing up outside and inside arms alternately, turn face and body each time.

25. First, back to back, swing over outside and inside arms alternately, twice each, simultaneously three times.

26. First, turn face to face with outside arms ; second, back to back with outside arms ; same with inside arms, etc.

FOURTH SET.

27. First, left face ; second, left feet together ; third, swing hands over head and step forward with right foot, bend and straighten right knees.

28. Same movement with right feet together.

FIFTH SET.

29. First, face to face, step alternately right feet diagonally forward to left of partner, and left feet to right.

RINGS IN QUARTETTES.

Music — "*Wine, Woman, and Song.*"

Stand facing each other, hands joined, and on first strain couples next platform raise hands and second couple pass under.

Rings on shoulders for the rest of strain. Hands toward platform up four times, towards sides room four times, alternate four times, together four; stamp left foot, then right, charge right in front of nose, bending and straightening right knee, raise and lower arms.

Rings on shoulder, out, four times front, four sides, alternate four, together four.

Charge left foot.

Rings on shoulder, down, four times front, four sides, alternate four, together four. Charge through one strain right foot, through one strain left.

Rings down. Bring above head, front four, sides four, alternate four, together four; charge double time without stamping, twice ends, twice sides, alternate one strain.

INDIAN CLUBS.

These exercises differ from the others inasmuch as the move_ments are to be taken slowly. If performed too rapidly they can never be well learned or executed.

The head and body should be held firmly erect, the handle of club grasped firmly, extending the thumb along the shank, which will enable one to control the movements of the club more easily.   The wrist must be slightly bent in order to make the arm and club quite straight ; if the club is held perpendicular, let it be *exactly* so ; if held horizontal, exactly horizontal. In the half arm and side circle movements the grasp must be a little relaxed to facilitate the perfect circle.

Accuracy is of the first importance, but difficult to secure in exercises with clubs.   Patience is required, especially in exercising with the left hand in the circles, where great flexibility of wrist joint is necessary.

CLUB EXERCISES.

Music — "*Sans Souci.*"

March in with clubs on shoulders.   March forward in four lines and arrange in quartettes.

1st signal.   Clubs down.

2d signal.   Clubs extended right and left.

3d signal.   Turn facing side of room.

4th signal.   Extend clubs right and left, to measure distances.

5th signal.   Back to position, with clubs down at sides.

1   Raise clubs to horizontal, right twice, left twice, alternate twice, together twice.

2. Clubs remain horizontal ; raise above head to perpendicular ; right twice, left twice, alternate twice, together twice.

3. Diagonal alternate circle forward over shoulder, right club first.

4. Charges.

In each charge rest two counts, charge two counts.   Diagonal charge toward partner, letting club drop upon arm.

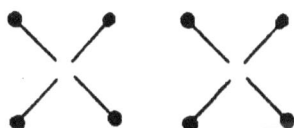

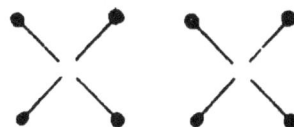

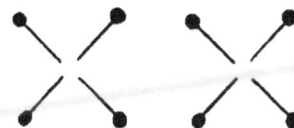

FIRST CHARGE. **SECOND CHARGE.**

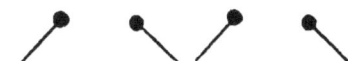

THIRD CHARGE. **FOURTH CHARGE.**

5. Diagonal alternate circle backward over shoulder.

6. Wing charges.

First count, bring clubs to horizontal in front, clubs up, rest one count " two and."

Charge to right (three and), rest (four and).

Charge to left (five and), rest (six and).

Charge to right (seven and), rest (eight and).

Charge to left (one and), rest (two and).

Charge to right (three and), rest (four and).

Charge to left (five and).

On six, turn one-eighth to center of room, raise clubs diagonally up, keep parallel through (seven and) (eight and).

7. Large circle backward (eight counts) ; large circle forward (eight counts).

8. Upon and after the eighth count, turn to position (face front) and place right club perpendicularly up, left perpendicularly down. Small circle back of head with right hand through four counts, straightening arm above head on every "and." Same left, changing on "and" after eight.

9. On "and" after eight, both clubs rest on shoulders. One small front side circle, on "and" step directly in front, clubs down in line with body. On two, small backward side circle to position, on "and" clubs on shoulders ; same left ; repeat, through eight counts.

10. Alternate small circles back of shoulder, over four counts, on "and" both clubs perpendicular over head, both arms straight.

11. Large wholly front parallel circle to right, eight counts ; same to left, eight counts.

12. Alternate small circles back of shoulder, under, four counts.

13. Wheel. Large circle, left hand front, small circle, right hand back, at same time ; hands changed ; eight counts.

14. Small and large circles crossing, first back of head, then large circle in front ; eight counts.

15. Small parallel circle back of head from left to right, large parallel circle from left to right in front, step diagonally back, turn right foot, clubs on shoulders on "two" ; on "and" small side front circles ; on "three" large parallel front circles from right to left ; on "and" small parallel circles back of head, from right to left ; on "four" large parallel front circles from right to left ; on "and" clubs on shoulders ; on "five" step diagonally back, turn left foot and repeat twice.

Repeat Nos. 13 and 14.

PERCUSSION.

It is well to conclude each lesson with percussion, as it is the best remedy for all lameness or soreness of muscle, of which beginners in Gymnastics often complain.

The pupils are arranged in couples, facing the same way, the one in front bending slightly forward with arms folded. The percussion occupies a whole strain. Instantly, at the end of the strain, they turn their faces in the opposite direction, and the percussion is repeated upon the other person. Percuss gently at first, and always alternate the blows. Never use hands simultaneously.

No. 1. Percuss shoulders. Reverse and repeat.

No. 2. Percuss small of back. Reverse and repeat.

No. 3. Percuss right side under uplifted arm. Reverse and repeat.

No. 4. Percuss left side. Reverse and repeat.

No. 5. Percuss both sides. Reverse and repeat.

No. 6. Percuss extended right arm, which is constantly turned from right to left. Reverse and repeat.

No. 7. Percuss extended left arm. Reverse and repeat.

No. 8. Percuss both arms. Reverse and repeat.

No. 9. Percuss chest, not too vigorously. Reverse and repeat.

MARCHES.

In marching take erect position in line, about two feet apart; turn square corners, and keep step with the music.

SINGLE FILE MARCH.

March about the hall, up and down, crossing from side to side, diagonally; march on tip-toe; on heels; on right toes and left heel; on left toes and right heel; without bending knees; bending knees; toes outward; toes inward; arms folded; arms folded behind; hands clasped back of head.

MAIN-SPRING MARCH.

Single file; wind up like a watch-spring, by leader going into the circle and keeping near to outside ring all the time; then unwind, leader turning and passing through the spaces of the previous winding, until a large circle is formed again.

EGYPTIAN PYRAMID MARCH.

Form a pyramid; first one person, behind her two persons, behind them three persons, and so on until all are taken. All are at one end of hall in center. Right face all; first one march off; when she gets to end of first couple, they follow; and so on till all are in single file.

WHEEL MARCH.

Each line forms a spoke of the wheel, those at the "hub" being the "end ones" of the lines; march close together, with very short steps. After turning two or three times around, the leader of first line marches slowly off in a tangent to the wheel, down the hall, followed by the end one from each "spoke." On the second revolution of the wheel, one from each spoke form a second line parallel with first, and so on until the class is formed in fours or eights abreast, as the case may be.

This may be repeated at the opposite end or sides of the hall.

DIAGONAL PLATOON MARCH.

March in two files on either side of room, halting at upper end and marking time ; No. 1 of file one marches diagonally across the space between lines, crossing to opposite corner ; when in middle of space, No. 1 of file two does the same, and so on until all have come down ; all are marching meanwhile, or marking time with feet. This may be done with twos, fours, eights, etc.

REGULAR, OR DOUBLE MARCH.

March in twos around outside of hall, then down center ; separate, and return to other end in single columns on either side ; march down in twos. At the lower end of hall, the first couple to right, second to left ; then come down in fours ; first four to right, second to left ; come down in eights ; then wheel in eights, at lower and upper end of hall. Then separate, fours to right, and fours to left ; come down in fours ; then in twos ; then single file.

March at arms' length, in couples. Join hands at upper end of hall, face each other, form arch. The second couple immediately skip under this arch and place themselves by the sides of the first couple, and put their arms up in the same position. The third couple do the same, and so on. As soon as all are thus placed, the head couple immediately join hands and skip down under the entire arch. The second couple do the same thing, and so on till all the couples have skipped through and return to the upper end of the hall, marching in single file on the outside.

Arriving at the head of the hall, instead of joining hands with partners, remain eight feet apart, and march down through hall thus separated. When the two lines are in position, join hands, and step quickly forward toward each other four beats, then step back again four beats. But the head couple, instead of retreating with the lines, join hands and skip rapidly down through the retreating lines, making their escape from the lines before the approaching lines catch them.   On the second approach the second couple join hands, and repeat what the first couple have just accomplished.   If the line be a long one, to prevent long waiting it is well to have two couples or three couples join hands and skip down at each approach of the two lines.

RING MARCH.

Many of the changes of the Single File and Double Marches may be introduced here.

Carry ring in right hand.   Join rings at upper end of hall and pull once, return and pull with other hand.   (In order to change hands it is well to change sides at the lower end of the hall.)   Push with right and left, then with both hands.

Form line on each side of hall, join rings, raise them high, and march or leap to center of room.   When the two lines are exactly opposite, drop hands to position ; all face quickly down the hall, and march single file till the lines are opposite again. Cross hands and repeat.

Skip down the hall, in couples, with the hands in front lowered, the other hands lifted.

March four abreast ; let two lines of couples march down the hall, the lines being eight feet apart.   When all are in these two parallel lines, suddenly stop and face towards the center.   Of course there will be a double row of persons on either side. Now let the two heads of the inside lines join hands, and skip down through the center, followed by each succeeding couple. When they reach the end of the hall let them separate and return just outside the lines left standing.   Let the inside lines repeat the figure and return to the outside of the first line. Now the heads of the four lines may join hands and skip down through the center and return the same way.

March down the hall, as in the last movement. Let the two inside lines join hands, making a circle. Outside lines the same. Now let the inside lines skip in the circle to the left four beats, and the outside lines at the same time skip to the right four beats. Instantly stopping with a smart stamp, let them reverse, bringing themselves into the same position that they were in before they began to skip in the circle. Now let the arms of the outside circle fall over the heads of the inside circle, forming what is called a " basket." Now four steps to the center of the circle, and four retreat. Again four steps to the center and four retreat.

Now, the foot and head of the lines drawing back a little and making straight lines, the preceding exercise may be repeated.

WAND MARCH.

The wand should be held in right hand, resting against right shoulder, left hand down at side.

For marching with wands, a combination of the Single File and Double Marches may be used.

Couples place wands together in front horizontally, leap down center with short or long step, then with long leaping step; leaping twice on right foot, almost directly at side, and lifting wands over head; then twice on left, bringing wands to front.

Couples separate at lower end of hall, marching up sides in single file; stop at upper corner and all face across the room; marking time with left foot, march across the hall, partners pass to the left of each other; reverse and repeat.

LEAPING AND SKIPPING.

These steps should be taken on toes.

Leaping.— Leap diagonally to the side, right and left, alternately, either with long or short steps. This may be repeated, hopping twice on either side.

Skipping.—This consists in sliding one foot before the other, either diagonally or at the side, bringing the other foot to right angle with it. Skip twice to right, twice to left.

Skip twice to right, then hop on right foot, then twice to left, hop on left foot. " Heel and toe " step may be taken, placing toe forward instead of heel. If in the Double March, hands may be crossed in front, or clasped and lifted high, otherwise hands should be on hips in taking these exercises.

MUSIC.

As the exercises are to be taken with energy, precision, and dash, the music should be distinctly marked, and that which may be easily understood. The simplest music is the best. In playing, the accented note is touched with much force, to accord with and mark the leading motion of the exercise.

For Free Gymnastics " *Captain Jinks* " or other well-marked and familiar music is desirable — marches, polkas, or galops.

For Dumb Bells, marches and waltzes.

For Wands, marches.

For Rings, waltzes.

A skillful musician can easily adapt Scotch airs and other familiar music for the Gymnasium.

Singing can be introduced with good effect.

GYMNASTIC APPARATUS.

The apparatus should be made of well-seasoned maple or black walnut.

The Dumb Bell should weigh about a pound; lobes three inches in diameter, and the handles should be in length what the lobes are in diameter.

Wands for ladies should be four feet long and three-quarters of an inch in diameter.

Rings should be made of three pieces of wood placed together, cross grain, six inches across on the outside, and one inch in diameter.

The Club should weigh about a pound, and should extend about two inches above elbow when held upon the arm extended horizontally.

Apparatus may be obtained of Wm. Fay, Chester, Mass.

THE GYMNASTIC DRESS.

The dress may be of flannel (dark blue is preferred), made with blouse-waist, loose belt, sleeves moderately full, good length, and closed at the wrist.

It requires about eight yards of flannel, single width, or four and a half double width, for the dress, including drawers, which may be pieced at the top with cambric.

The dress should not be trimmed heavily ; a flounce about six inches deep should be stitched on to the lower edge of the skirt, not put *on* the skirt, and a band of trimming to match collar and cuffs, or rows of braid, may be placed above the flounce.

Width of skirt about two and one fourth yards, and seven inches from floor.

The waist should be made long enough under the arms to allow the arms to be stretched upward to their utmost extent without drawing upon the belt at all. Shoulder seam should be short, and arm-holes large.

Corsets and high-heeled boots are out of place in the Gymnasium.

For books containing illustrations see Dr. Dio Lewis's *New Gymnastics for Men, Women, and Children*, published by Clarke Bros., Nos. 68 and 69 Bible House, New York ; *The Indian Club Exercise*, by Sim. D. Kehoe, published by Peck & Snyder, 124 Nassau St., New York.

www.ingramcontent.com/pod-product-compliance
Lightning Source LLC
Chambersburg PA
CBHW021456090426
42739CB00009B/1749